My Home Country

NICARAGUA

IS MY HOME

For a free color catalog describing Gareth Stevens' list of high-quality books, call 1-800-341-3569 (USA) or 1-800-461-9120 (Canada).

For their help in the preparation of *My Home Country: Nicaragua*, the editors gratefully thank the Sandinista Children's Association and Escuela Teresa Arce, León, Nicaragua; Project Minnesota-León; the Embassy of Nicaragua (Canada), Ottawa, Ontario; Professor Howard Handelman, University of Wisconsin-Milwaukee; and Professor Michael Fleet, Marquette University, Milwaukee.

Library of Congress Cataloging-in-Publication Data

Daniel, Jamie.
      Nicaragua is my home / adapted from Ronnie Cummins' Children of the world--Nicaragua by Jamie Daniel ; photographs by Rose Welch.
          p. cm. -- (My home country)
      Includes bibliographical references and index.
      Summary: A look at the life of a ten-year-old boy and his family living in a suburb of Leon, Nicaragua's second largest city. Includes a section with information on Nicaragua.
      ISBN 0-8368-0850-9
      1. Nicaragua--Social life and customs--Juvenile literature. [1. Family life--Nicaragua. 2. Nicaragua.] I. Welch, Rose, ill. II. Cummins, Ronnie. Nicaragua. III. Title. IV. Series.
F1523.8.D36   1992
972.8505--dc20   92-17723

Edited, designed, and produced by

Gareth Stevens Publishing
1555 North RiverCenter Drive, Suite 201
Milwaukee, Wisconsin 53212, USA

Text, photographs, and format copyright 1992 by Gareth Stevens, Inc. First published in the United States and Canada in 1992 by Gareth Stevens, Inc. This U.S. edition is abridged from *Children of the World: Nicaragua*, copyright 1990 by Gareth Stevens, Inc., with text by Ronnie Cummins and photographs by Rose Welch.

Series editor: Beth Karpfinger
Cover design: Kristi Ludwig
Designer: Laurie Shock
Map design: Sheri Gibbs

Printed in the United States of America

1 2 3 4 5 6 7 8 9 96 95 94 93 92

My Home Country

NICARAGUA

IS MY HOME

Adapted from Ronnie Cummins'
Children of the World: Nicaragua

by Jamie Daniel
Photographs by Rose Welch

Gareth Stevens Publishing
MILWAUKEE

Ten-year-old Michael Eduardo Chávez Garcia lives with his mother, grandparents, aunts, uncles, and cousins in San Jerónimo, a neighborhood on the outskirts of León, Nicaragua's second largest city. Although the homes in San Jerónimo are poor by North American standards, the people who live there feel that conditions are improving, and Michael enjoys being surrounded by so many friends and family members.

To enhance this book's value in libraries and classrooms, clear and simple reference sections include up-to-date information about Nicaragua's history, land and climate, people and language, education, and religion. *Nicaragua Is My Home* also features a large and colorful map, bibliography, glossary, simple index, and research topics and activity projects designed especially for young readers.

The living conditions and experiences of children in Nicaragua vary according to economic, environmental, and ethnic circumstances. The reference sections help bring to life for young readers the diversity and richness of the culture and heritage of Nicaragua. Of particular interest are discussions of Nicaragua since its revolution.

My Home Country includes the following titles:

Canada	*Nicaragua*
Costa Rica	*Peru*
Cuba	*Poland*
El Salvador	*South Africa*
Guatemala	*Vietnam*
Ireland	*Zambia*

CONTENTS

LIVING IN NICARAGUA:
   Michael, a Boy from León 7

At Home in the Barrio 10
Michael's School 16
After School 22
A Walk Around León 24
The Giant Puppets of León 30
Going to Market 32
Time Out for Sports 34
A Trip to the Pacific Ocean 36
Sunday Afternoon at Home 40

FOR YOUR INFORMATION: Nicaragua 42

Official Name 42
Capital 42
History 42
Land and Climate 43
People and Language 43
Education 43
Religion 44
Sports and Recreation 44
Currency 44
Nicaraguans in North America 44
Glossary 45
More Books About Nicaragua 45
Things To Do 45
Map of Nicaragua 46
Index 48

Michael (lower right) with his mother (far right) and some of the 34 relatives that live in their neighborhood.

North America

Nicaragua

South America

Europe

Africa

Asia

Australia

Republic of Nicaragua

Mexico

Caribbean Sea

Belize

Honduras

León

Guatemala

El Salvador

Costa Rica

Pacific Ocean

Panama

LIVING IN NICARAGUA:
Michael, a Boy from León

Michael Eduardo Chávez Garcia is ten years old. He lives in a city in Nicaragua called León. It is the second-largest city in the country, with more than 130,000 people.

Like most children in Nicaragua, Michael lives near many of his relatives. Their street is named Chávez Street, after Michael's father. He was killed in the revolutionary war in Nicaragua before Michael was born.

From a rooftop, Michael looks out over León.

7

León is one of the oldest cities in Nicaragua.

A vendor's horse-drawn cart passes Michael's home.

At Home in the Barrio

Michael's family has lived in the same neighborhood, or *barrio*, for the last 22 years. Since so many cousins live close by, Michael can always find someone to play with.

Many children in North America might think that Michael and his family are poor. Most people in Nicaragua don't have cars, air conditioners, or even fans.

Michael and his cousins play in the courtyard of the Chávez home.

But conditions in Nicaragua are improving, and the children are happy and healthy.

Many families in the barrio own their home.
But Michael's family of nine rent the house
they live in. Although they are crowded,
they are content in their five-room home.

The house is simple but comfortable. There
is no television or phone. In the barrio, no
one has a private phone. A public phone
sits outside the Chávez home. Everyone in
the neighborhood uses it.

The street on which Michael lives was named after his father.

Above: Michael's house is simple inside as well as outside. Below: Michael buys a treat from a *tienda*, or store.

There are no big stores in the barrio. Another family runs a small store called a *tienda* in its front room. Here, Michael buys homemade candy and cool drinks.

Everyone gets up early in the Chávez house to help prepare breakfast and get ready for school. In the early morning, it is much cooler than the rest of the day, and it is easier to get daily chores done.

After eating a filling breakfast of rice, beans, and fried bananas, Michael and his mother take the same bus to school and work.

Michael's grandmother works hard to prepare corn tortillas for the family. First, she grinds the corn. Then she mixes it into a dough. The dough is patted into a round, flat cake and baked over an open fire.

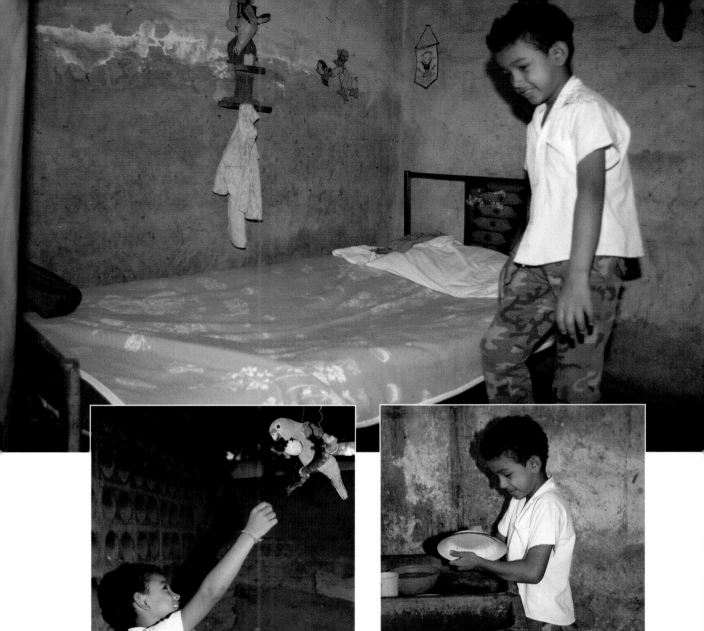

Michael makes his bed, feeds his pet parrot, "Laura", and helps with washing dishes.

Michael poses with his fourth-grade class.

Michael's School

Michael is in fourth grade at a school called Escuela Teresa Arce. *Escuela* means "school" in Spanish. Many members of Michael's family have also attended this school.

Michael likes history and math best. He works hard in class and at home. He is one of the better students in his class.

Left: Michael works hard on his math homework.
Below: Here are some of the textbooks he uses at school.

Michael and his classmates take turns reading out loud.

History is a subject that is stressed at Escuela Teresa Arce. The city of León has a long history that the children must study. León was founded in 1524 and is one of the oldest cities in the Americas.

In order to make the few school buildings less crowded, some children go to school in the morning and others go in the afternoon. Michael likes to go to the early classes so that he has the rest of the day to play at home.

Most children in Nicaragua wear uniforms to school. These girls wear a white blouse and a dark skirt ▶

Michael's class has recess at 9:30 a.m. The children can run out into the courtyard and let out some energy after sitting at their desks all morning.

A physical education teacher leads the children in sports and exercises three times a week. Michael's favorite sport is baseball.

Left: The children have recess in the sunny courtyard.
Below: Physical education is a subject all the children enjoy.

When Michael comes home from school, one of his jobs is to water the plants on the family patio.

Inset photo: Michael's mother works in an office near Michael's school.

After School

Michael's mother works at the Children's Association. Her job is to keep records of the association's expenses. Michael walks to his mother's office when school gets out, and together, they ride the bus back home.

After they have lunch together, Mrs. Chávez must go back to work. But Michael can stay at home and play after he's finished his home-work and chores.

Right: Michael and his cousin Kelvin ride together on Kelvin's bicycle.
Below: Michael and Kelvin also like to play checkers — here, Michael makes a winning jump.

A Walk Around León

Michael, his mother, and his younger cousins are taking weekend tours of León as part of a school history project. They start their tour in the city's central park.

The first stop is the Indian neighborhood of Subtiava, where Michael and his cousins explore the crumbling ruins of the church of Vera Cruz.

Cabs drawn by horses take people all over the city of León. It's a slower ride than a car or bus but much more fun!

Above: The children explore a ruin on their walking tour of León. One of their favorite spots is the old church at Vera Cruz.

Right: The church of Santa Lucia was built by Spanish colonists in 1530.

The children play in the shade of El Tamarindo.

The next stop in Subtiava is the giant old tree called El Tamarindo. The tree is more than 200 years old. A rebel Indian chief was once hanged from the tree by the Spanish.

Top: The cathedral in León is in the center of the city.
Inset, left: The children climb on the stone lions that stand guard outside. *León* means "lion" in Spanish.
Inset, right: The cathedral contains many huge oil paintings like this one.

Next, Michael and his family visit the Roman Catholic cathedral at León. It is the largest church in Central America. Two big stone lions guard the church's altar.

27

Above: This burned-out
building was a jail during the
Nicaraguan war.
Right: A statue of a rebel
fighter stands outside
the ruin.

At the end of the tour, ruins remind the
family of the 1979 uprising in which Mr.
Chávez was killed. That year, the
Nicaraguan people fought and defeated the
troops of the dictator, Anastasio Somoza.

Michael's father and over 40,000 other Nicaraguans lost their lives in the fight for freedom. Some of the ruins where the worst fighting took place still stand, serving as constant reminders of León's history.

Many buildings were destroyed during the battles in 1979. All that is left of this building is an archway.

The Giant Puppets of León

Las Gigantonas, or giant puppets, have been a tradition in León for hundreds of years. The puppets were first made by Indians to poke fun at the Spanish who colonized Nicaragua.

A local woman, 71-year-old Doña Carmen Toruno de Garcia, makes the puppets and trains new puppet artists to carry on the special tradition.

Above: Doña Garcia is proud of the tradition she keeps alive. Below: A giant puppet dances in the street.

Doña Carmen shows off some of her wonderful puppets.

Going to Market

Michael's grandfather grows some of the family's food on a plot of land outside the city. But there are still some things the family needs to buy. Mrs. Chávez does her shopping at a big outdoor market in the middle of León. Here, she can buy fresh fruits and vegetables.

Vendors also sell clothing, flowers, and homemade soap. Michael likes to go with his mother to the market.

Mrs. Chávez buys fresh fruit.

Most Nicaraguans eat simple foods such as red beans, rice, onions, tomatoes, corn tortillas, and plantains, a type of banana. Meat is too expensive to eat every day.

Top: Canned goods can also be
bought at the market.
Insets: Vendors sell bread
(left) and fresh flowers (right).

The favorite dish of most Nicaraguans is
gallo-pinto, a mixture of rice and red beans
that is fried with diced onions and spices.

Michael and his friends like to play marbles.

Time Out for Sports

León has many sports teams. Basketball, soccer, volleyball, and baseball are popular.

Many children play sports on junior league teams. On the weekends, every park and vacant lot in León has a game going on.

Right: People in León often play volleyball in spite of the hot weather.
Below: Michael's baseball team is proud to pose for the camera.

Going to the beach is worth the trip on a crowded bus.

A Trip to the Pacific Ocean

Michael and Kelvin are excited to be going to the beach at Poneloya, a small fishing village eleven miles (17.5 km) away from the barrio. The bus is crowded, but Michael and his family don't mind. They are glad to be getting away from the hot city.

The family goes to
the southern end of
Poneloya. The water
is calm and shallow.
Michael and his
cousins can swim
and play here safely.

Right: Ahh . . . Cool water!
Below: Sand hopscotch.

After a quiet day at the beach, León seems noisy and crowded.

Sunday Afternoon at Home

Michael's relatives get together on Sunday afternoons. After working hard all week, Michael's aunts and uncles are happy to just sit and relax.

Everyone is looking forward to the rainy season, when it gets cool and everything turns deep green. Michael smiles as he remembers the sound of rain on the roof.

Michael's grandfather likes to play checkers.
Below: Even the children like to sit and relax for a while.

Michael holds his baby cousin, Zuleyka.

MORE FACTS ABOUT: Nicaragua

Official Name: Republica de Nicaragua

(ray-POOH-blee-kah DAY nee-kuh-RAHG-wha)
Republic of Nicaragua

Capital: Managua (mah-NOG-wha)

History

Indians were the original inhabitants of Nicaragua. The Spanish arrived in the 16th century and used their superior force to conquer the Indians.

Long after Nicaragua gained independence from Spain, it was governed by dictators who jailed or killed their opponents. The most powerful attempt to gain freedom was led between 1927 and 1933 by Augusto Cesar Sandino. Dictator Anastasio Somoza defeated Sandino and his rebels.

Somoza ruled for many years. To oppose him, people formed the Sandinista Front for National Liberation. The Sandinistas began a revolution against Somoza in 1979. In five years of fighting, 40,000 people died, but Somoza was finally defeated. Democratic elections were held in 1984. Sandinistan Daniel Ortega became the new president. He was replaced by Violeta Barrios de Chamorro in 1990.

Land and Climate

Nicaragua is the largest country in Central America. It is about as big as Georgia in the US, and somewhat larger than the Canadian provinces of Nova Scotia and New Brunswick combined. Honduras lies to the north, Costa Rica to the south.

Nicaragua is a tropical country. It rains up to 240 inches (610 cm) every summer. The rest of the year is dry and hot. Farmers on the Pacific side of the country harvest their crops during the rainy season. Farmers in the mountains grow coffee, the country's major export.

People and Language

3.3 million people live in Nicaragua. Most are *mestizos*, people whose ancestors were both Spanish and Indian. About 8% are black, and 4% Indian.

The official language of Nicaragua is Spanish, but Creole and Indian are also spoken. English is taught in the schools.

Education

Before the Sandinista revolution, only half of the Nicaraguan people could read and write. Now twice as many children attend school than before the revolution. Only one out of ten Nicaraguans cannot read and write.

Religion

Most Nicaraguans are Roman Catholics, but there are also Protestant and Jewish Nicaraguans. Many people active in religious life were also Sandinista supporters. Church leaders still play an important part in the country's government.

Sports and Recreation

Baseball is the Nicaraguan national sport. Nicaraguans love to play and watch baseball. Many also play soccer, volleyball, basketball, and other sports. Both men and women participate.

A 5,000-córdoba note.

Nicaraguans in North America

About 250,000 Nicaraguans live in the United States. There are more Nicaraguans in Miami than any city in the world except Managua! Nicaraguans also live in Canada.

Glossary

barrio: A Spanish word for "neighborhood."

dictator: A ruler who has all of the power. Dictators often rule a country in a cruel way.

revolution: A complete change in government or rule after a violent struggle.

tienda: A small store run from a neighborhood home in Nicaragua.

More Books About Nicaragua

Nicaragua in Pictures. (Lerner Publications)
Nicaragua: Struggling with Change. Adams
  (Dillon Press)

Things To Do

1. For a Nicaraguan pen pal write to: Worldwide Pen Friends, P.O. Box 39097, Downey, CA 90241.

2. Nicaragua is home to several Indian tribes. At your library, find out about these tribes. How is tribal life in Central America different from that of Indian tribes in the United States and Canada?

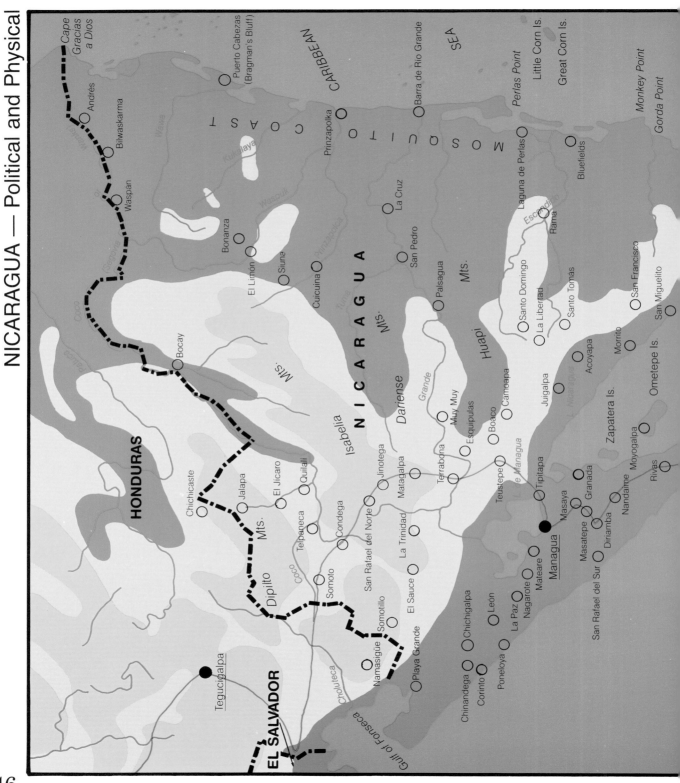

NICARAGUA — Political and Physical

Cape Gracias a Dios
Andrés
Bilwaskarma
Waspán
Puerto Cabezas (Bragman's Bluff)
Bilwaskarma
CARIBBEAN SEA
Barra de Rio Grande
Little Corn Is.
Great Corn Is.
Monkey Point
Gorda Point
Perlas Point
Prinzapolka
Laguna de Perlas
Bluefields
Rama
Escondido
MOSQUITO COAST
Wawa
Kukalaya
Waspuk
La Cruz
San Pedro
Palsagua
Santo Domingo
San Francisco
Santo Tomás
San Miguelito
Morrito
Acoyapa
Bonanza
El Limón
Siuna
Cuicuina
Prinzapolka
Tuma
NICARAGUA
Grande
Mts.
Dariense Mts.
Huapi Mts.
La Libertad
Jugalpa
Camoapa
Boaco
Muy Muy
Esquipulas
Matagalpa
Terrabona
Teustepe
Tipitapa
Ometepe Is.
Moyogalpa
Rivas
Zapatera Is.
Nandaime
Diriamba
Granada
Masaya
Masatepe
Lake Managua
Managua
Mateare
San Rafael del Sur
Nagarote
La Paz
León
Chichigalpa
Chinandega
Corinto
Poneloya
Playa Grande
Namasigue
Somotillo
Somoto
El Sauce
La Trinidad
San Rafael del Norte
Condega
Telpaneca
Quilalí
El Jícaro
Jinotega
Jalapa
Chichicaste
Bocay
Isabelia Mts.
Dipilto Mts.
Coco
HONDURAS
Tegucigalpa
EL SALVADOR
Gulf of Fonseca
Choluteca
Coco
Bocay
Segovia
Patuca

46

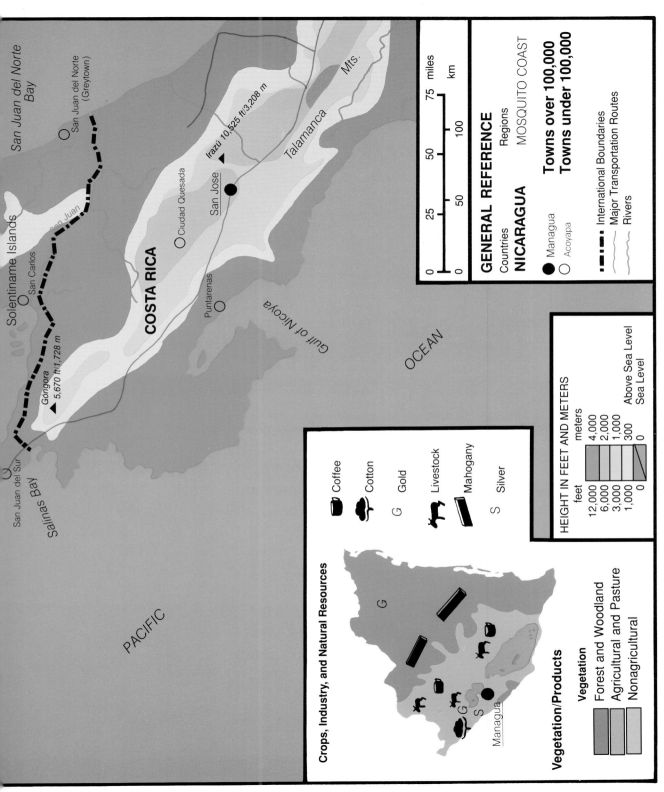

San Juan del Norte Bay

San Juan del Norte (Greytown)

Solentiname Islands

San Juan

San Carlos

Góngora
▲ 5,670 ft/1,728 m

San Juan del Sur

Salinas Bay

COSTA RICA

Ciudad Quesada

Puntarenas

San Jose

Irazú 10,525 ft/3,208 m ▲

Talamanca Mts.

Gulf of Nicoya

PACIFIC

OCEAN

GENERAL REFERENCE

Countries
NICARAGUA

Regions
MOSQUITO COAST

● Managua
○ Acoyapa

Towns over 100,000
Towns under 100,000

▪–▪–▪ International Boundaries
—— Major Transportation Routes
～～ Rivers

miles
km

0   25   50   75

0   50   100

HEIGHT IN FEET AND METERS

feet   meters
12,000   4,000
6,000   2,000
3,000   1,000
1,000   300
0   0

Above Sea Level
Sea Level

Crops, Industry, and Natural Resources

Coffee
Cotton
G Gold
Livestock
Mahogany
S Silver

G

G
S

Managua

Vegetation/Products

Vegetation

Forest and Woodland
Agricultural and Pasture
Nonagricultural

Index

barrio 10, 12, 36, 45

Canada 44
Central America 27, 43
Chamorro, Violeta Barrios de 42
Children's Association 22
climate 43

democracy 42
dictatorship 42, 45

El Tamarindo 26
elections 42
English 43
ethnic groups
    blacks 43
    Indians 43
    mestizos 43

food 13, 14, 32, 33, 43

Georgia 43

history 42
homework 23

Indians 24, 26, 42

land 43
language 43
Las Gigantonas 30
León 7, 8, 18, 24, 25, 27, 29, 32, 35

markets 32

New Brunswick 43
North America 10
Nova Scotia 43

Ortega Saavedra, Daniel 42

Pacific Ocean 36, 43
people 43
Poneloya 36, 37
president 42

revolution, Sandinista 7, 28, 29, 42, 43
religion 27, 44

Sandinista Front for National Liberation 42
Sandino, Augusto César 42
school and education 14, 16-22
Somoza, Anastasio 28, 42
Spain (Spanish) 16, 25, 26, 27, 30, 42-43
sports 21, 34, 44
    baseball 21, 34, 35, 44
    basketball 34, 44
    soccer 34, 44
    volleyball 34, 35, 44
Subtiava 24, 26

United States 43, 44

Vera Cruz 24, 25